15th Anniversary Limited Edition

BEST LOVED
Timeless Quilts

from the editors of *Traditional Quiltworks* and *Quilting Today* magazines

To Kathy,
With love,
Judi

CHITRA PUBLICATIONS

Your Best Value in Quilting

website: www.QuiltTownUSA.com

Chitra Publications
2 Public Avenue
Montrose, Pennsylvania 18801-1220

First printing: 2002

Library of Congress Cataloging-in-Publication Data

Best loved timeless quilts/from the editors of Traditional quiltworks & Quilting today magazines.
    p. cm.
  ISBN 1-885588-42-9
  1. Patchwork—Patterns. 2. Appliqué—Patterns. 3. Quilting. 4. Quilts. I. Title: Timeless quilts. II. Traditional quiltworks. III. Quilting today.

TT835 .B3624 2002
746.46'041—dc21

2001047757

Edited by: Elsie Campbell
Design & Illustrations: Brenda Pytlik
Cover Photography: Guy Cali Associates, Inc., Clark Summit, Pennsylvania
Inside Photography: VanZandbergen Photography, Brackney, Pennsylvania

Our Mission Statement:
We publish quality quilting magazines and books that recognize, promote, and inspire self-expression. We are dedicated to serving our customers with respect, kindness, and efficiency.

www.QuiltTownUSA.com

Introduction

From beginners to experienced quiltmakers and from rotary cutting and assembly-line piecing to fine hand appliqué, this book has something for everyone. Each quilt is a full-sized classic. We've gathered these special quilts together here in one convenient, easy-to-use pattern book you're sure to enjoy.

Pull out all those fat quarters that you've been collecting. Swap fabric swatches with friends, or unearth the boxes of scraps in the sewing room closet, and make scrap quilts like "Turkey Tracks", "Postage Stamp", or "Cabin Circles". Fabricaholics are sure to love combining lots of different prints and solids in these and the other tradition-

with-a-twist patterns contained on these pages. If appliqué is your preference, reproduce "Basket Bouquet", a historical design from the 1870's. Rotary cutting fans will find it simple to turn only 5 different fabrics into a stunning "Underground Railroad" quilt.

Spanning several generations of quiltmaking tradition, these "Best Loved Quilts" are sure to spark your imagination and satisfy your desire to create something wonderful. We invite you to begin a quilt today that is destined to become your family's heirloom tomorrow. Just turn this page, and get started!

The editorial team of Traditional Quiltworks *and* Quilting Today *magazines, clockwise from the top: Debra Feece, Sherry Bonnice, Joyce Libal, Deborah Hearn, Jack Braunstein, and Elsie Campbell.*

Table of Contents

Basket Bouquet

Reproduce an appliqué design from 1870.

QUILT SIZE: 42" square

MATERIALS
- Fat eighth (11" x 18") dark red print
- Fat quarter (18" x 22") dark green print
- Fat quarter sage green print
- Fat eighth olive green print
- Fat eighth gray/green print
- Fat eighth pink plaid
- 2" x 6" strip orange print
- Fat eighth brown plaid
- Fat eighth turquoise plaid
- 1/4 yard blue print
- 1 1/4 yards tan print
- 1 5/8 yards blue check
- 1 1/2 yards backing fabric
- 46" square of batting
- Green embroidery floss

CUTTING
The pattern pieces are on page 24. Appliqué pieces are full size and do not include a turn-under allowance. Make templates for each of the pieces. Trace around the templates on the right side of the fabric and add a 1/8" x 3 /16" turn-under allowance when cutting the pieces out. All other dimensions include a 1/4" seam allowance.
For the flowers, berries, leaves, and basket:
- Cut 2: A-1, dark green print
- Cut 2: A-2, dark red print
- Cut 3: B-2, dark red print
- Cut 12: berries, dark red print
- Cut 2: B-1, gray/green print
- Cut 1: B-1, olive green print
- Cut 3: B-3, pink plaid
- Cut 3: B-4, orange print
- Cut 10: leaves, 2 from each print to match the corresponding stem
- Cut 1: flower basket, brown plaid
For the stems and basket handles:
- Cut 2: 1" x 8 1/2" bias strips, turquoise plaid

- Cut 2: 1 1/4" x 11 1/2" bias strips, gray/green print
- Cut 2: 1 1/4" x 8 1/2" bias strips, dark green print
- Cut 1: 1 1/4" x 11 1/2" bias strip, olive green print
- Cut 2: 1" x 3 1/2" bias strips, brown plaid, for the flower basket handles
Also:
- Cut 6: 5 3/4" squares, blue print
- Cut 1: 5 3/4" square, dark green print
- Cut 1: 5 3/4" square, turquoise plaid
- Cut 8: 5 3/4" squares, tan print
- Cut 1: 29" square, tan print, for the background
- Cut 2: 5" x 33" strips, blue check, for the borders
- Cut 2: 5" x 42" strips, blue check, for the borders
- Cut 1: 36" square, blue check, then cut 2 1/2"-wide bias strips and join them to make a long bias binding strip at least 175"

DIRECTIONS
- Press under a 1/4" seam allowance on the long sides of each bias strip. Set them aside.
- Fold the 29" tan print square in half vertically and crease the fold. Open the square.
- For the center stem, pin the prepared olive bias strip along the crease. Pin the 2 olive leaves, the olive B-1, a dark red print B-2, a pink plaid B-3, an orange print B-4, and the flower basket to the quilt, referring to the quilt photo.
- Appliqué all the pieces, except the flower basket, in the order given, turning the edges under with the point of your needle as you stitch. Do not turn under the allowance or stitch where pieces are overlapped by other appliqués.
- Referring to the quilt photo for placement, lay out the prepared gray/green bias

strips, the matching leaves, the matching B-1's, and the remaining B-2's, B-3's, and B-4's and pin them in place.
- Appliqué the pieces in order, as before, tucking the ends of the bias strips under the flower basket.
- Pin the prepared dark green print bias strips, matching leaves, A-2's, and A-1's on the quilt. Tuck one end of the prepared 1" x 8 1/2" turquoise bias strips under the dark green strips. Appliqué the pieces.
- Pin the berries on the quilt and appliqué them in place.
- For the flower basket handles, pin the prepared brown bias strips to the quilt, tucking the ends under the side edges of the basket. Appliqué them in place.
- Appliqué the flower basket to the background.
- Using a chain stitch, embroider lines connecting each berry to the bias stems.
- Trim the square to 28 1/2".

For the Pieced Border:
- Use a pencil to draw diagonal lines from corner to corner on the wrong side of each 5 3/4" tan print square. Then draw horizontal and vertical lines through the centers.
- Lay a marked tan print square on a 5 3/4" blue print square, right sides together. Stitch 1/4" away from both sides of the diagonal lines, as shown. Make 6.
- In the same manner, place a marked tan print square on a 5 3/4" dark green print square and stitch 1/4" away from both sides of the diagonal lines.
- Place a marked tan print square on a 5 3/4" turquoise plaid square and stitch 1/4" away from both sides of the diagonal lines.

"Basket Bouquet" *(42" square) was stitched by Rose Wiebe Haury of Topeka, Kansas. Make your own interpretation of this delightful wallhanging which was inspired by an antique quilt from the 1870's. The sawtooth border is in keeping with the style of that era.*

• Cut the squares on the drawn lines to yield 64 pieced squares. You will use 60.

• Lay out an assortment of 14 pieced squares, half going in one direction and half in the opposite direction, as shown. Join them to make a pieced border. Make 2.

• Stitch the pieced borders to opposite sides of the quilt, placing the tan print against the quilt.

• Lay out 16 pieced squares in the same manner and stitch them together to make a long pieced border. Make 2.

• Stitch the long pieced borders to the remaining sides of the quilt.

• Measure the length of the quilt. Trim the 5" x 33" blue check strips to that measurement. Stitch them to the sides of the quilt.

• Measure the width of the quilt, including the borders. Trim the 5" x 42" blue check strips to that measurement. Stitch them to the top and bottom of the quilt.

• Using a plate or other round object as a guide, draw a curved edge on each corner of the quilt. Trim on the line.

• Finish the quilt as described in the *General Directions,* using the 2 1/2"-wide blue check bias strips for the binding.

(The full-size pattern pieces are on page 24.)

Underground Railroad

Let this antique strippy quilt inspire today's traditions in your family.

*Joyce E. Harvill, of Johnson City, Tennessee, is the proud owner of "**Underground Railroad**" (69" x 80"). This quilt has been passed down through five generations of her family. It was made by her great-great-grandmother, Catherine Ulmer, in 1898. Your version of this simple but dramatic quilt is sure to become a treasured heirloom in your own family.*

QUILT SIZE: 69" x 80"
BLOCK SIZE: 8" square

MATERIALS
- 1 yard off-white print
- 1 3/4 yards green print
- 1 yard pink print
- 1 yard blue print

NOTE: *Catherine Ulmer used black print for some of the blocks in her quilt. These directions are for blue print in all of the blocks. If you wish to include black in your quilt, you will need 1/8 yard of black print for 4 blocks.*

- 2 3/4 yards red print
- 4 1/4 yards backing fabric
- 73" x 84" piece of batting

CUTTING
- Cut 42: 4 7/8" squares, off-white print
- Cut 42: 4 7/8" squares, green print
- Cut 8: 2 1/2" x 44" strips, green print, for the binding
- Cut 11: 2 1/2" x 44" strips, pink print
- Cut 11: 2 1/2" x 44" strips, blue print

NOTE: *If you choose to use black print for some blocks, cut 10 blue strips and one black strip.*

- Cut 6: 12 5/8" squares, red print, then cut them in quarters diagonally to yield 24 setting triangles. You will use 22.
- Cut 30: 8 1/2" squares, red print
- Cut 2: 6 5/8" squares, red print, then cut them in half diagonally to yield 4 corner triangles

DIRECTIONS
- Draw a diagonal line from corner to corner on the wrong side of each 4 7/8" off-white print square.
- Place a marked off-white print square on a 4 7/8" green print square, right sides together. Stitch 1/4" away from the drawn line on both sides, as shown, Make 42.
- Cut the squares on the drawn lines to yield 84 pieced squares. Press the seam allowances toward the green print. Set them aside.
- Stitch a 2 1/2" x 44" pink print strip to a 2 1/2" x 44" blue print strip, right sides

together along their length, to make a pieced panel. Make 11.
• Cut one hundred sixty-eight 2 1/2" slices from the pieced panels.
• Stitch two 2 1/2" slices together to form a Four Patch, as shown. Make 84.
• Lay out 2 Four Patches and 2 pieced

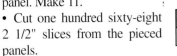

squares in 2 rows of 2. Join them to make a block, as shown. Make 42.

ASSEMBLY

• Referring to the quilt photo for placement, lay out the blocks in diagonal rows alternating them with the 8 1/2" red print squares. Place the red print setting triangles

along the outer edges and the red print corner triangles at the corners.
• Stitch the blocks, red print squares, and triangles into diagonal rows and join the rows.
• Finish the quilt as described in the *General Directions*, using the 2 1/2" x 44" green print strips for the binding.

Cabin Circles

Make easy Log Cabin blocks that dance in circles across this quilt.

Log Cabin-style quilts have been around for generations and every quilter wants to make at least one. The beauty of this unique design belies it's simple construction methods. Scraps left over from other projects found their way into Kaye DeMars' "Cabin Circles" (49" x 59"). The Ft. Myers, Florida, resident decided to quilt more circles inside the Log Cabin block groups and chose a simple cable design for the border quilting.

QUILT SIZE: 49" x 59"
BLOCK SIZE: 5" square

MATERIALS
• Assorted light prints ranging in size from 1" x 9" to 1" x 44" and totaling 1 1/4 yards
• Assorted dark prints ranging in size from 1 1/2" x 13" to 1 1/2" x 44" and totaling 2 yards
• Assorted red prints each at least 1" x 9" and totaling 1/4 yard
• 3/4 yard blue print for the border
• 1/2 yard black print for the binding
• 3 yards backing fabric
• 53" x 63" piece of batting

CUTTING
• Cut 10: 1" x 9" strips, assorted light prints
• Cut 10: 1" x 13" strips, assorted light prints
• Cut 30: 1" x 44" strips, assorted light prints
• Cut 10: 1 1/2" x 13" strips, assorted dark prints
• Cut 40: 1 1/2" x 44" strips, assorted dark prints
• Cut 10: 1" x 9" strips, assorted red prints

(Continued on page 25)

Christmas Stars

This festive wall quilt lends joy to the holiday season.

QUILT SIZE: 40 1/2" square
BLOCK SIZE: 7 1/4" square

MATERIALS
- 1/2 yard red print for the stars
- 1/2 yard light print for the Star block backgrounds
- 1 yard large floral
- 1/2 yard dark green solid
- 3/4 yard green print for the border and binding
- 1 1/4 yards backing fabric
- 45" square of batting

CUTTING
Pattern piece B is on page 28. Pattern pieces are full size and include a 1/4" seam allowance, as do all dimensions given.
- Cut 64: A, red print
- Cut 8: 4 1/4" squares, light print, then cut them in quarters diagonally to yield 32 triangles
- Cut 32: 2 5/8" squares, light print
- Cut 2: 11 1/4" squares, large floral, then cut them in half diagonally to yield 4 corner triangles
- Cut 8: B, large floral
- Cut 8: B, dark green solid
- Cut 4: 2 3/4" x 44" strips, green print, for the border
- Cut 4: 2 1/2" x 44" strips, green print, for the binding

DIRECTIONS
For each of 8 Star blocks:
- Stitch 2 red print A's together into a pair, as shown, backstitching at the dots. Make 4.

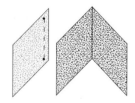

- Set a 2 5/8" light print square into a pair, as shown. Make 4.

- Stitch 2 units together to make a half-star. Make 2.

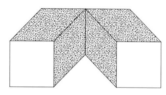

- Stitch the half-stars together to make a star.
- Set 4 light print triangles into the star to complete a Star block. Make 8.

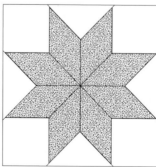

ASSEMBLY
- In the same manner as for the Star blocks, stitch 2 large floral B's together into a pair, backstitching at the dots. Make 4.
- Stitch 2 pairs together to make a half-star. Make 2.
- Join the half-stars to make the Center Star.
- Referring to the quilt photo, set the Star blocks into the Center Star.
- Set in the dark green B's between the outer edges of the Star blocks.
- Stitch a large floral triangle to each corner of the quilt. Trim the corners to square the quilt, if necessary.
- Measure the length of the quilt. Trim 2 of the 2 3/4" x 44" green print strips to that measurement. Stitch them to opposite sides of the quilt.
- Measure the width of the quilt, including the borders. Trim the remaining 2 3/4" x 44" green print strips to that measurement. Stitch them to the remaining sides of the quilt.
- Finish the quilt as described in the *General Directions,* using the 2 1/2" x 44" green print strips for the binding.

Full-size pattern piece A for Christmas Stars. Pattern piece B is on page 28.

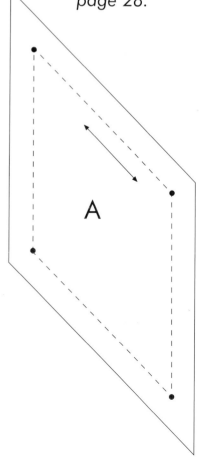

"Christmas Stars" (40 1/2" square) adds to the festive holiday atmosphere in Barbara Flowers' home in Medina, Ohio. Barbara used two high contrasting fabrics for the stars to give them visual impact. A large floral print completes the quilt beautifully. Stitch your own version of this high-contrast Christmas quilt, and enjoy it all year long!

My Consolation

Quick and easy describes this winner!

QUILT SIZE: 90" x 105"
BLOCK SIZE: 7 1/2" square

MATERIALS
- Light print scraps, each at least 3" square and totaling 2 1/3 yards
- Dark print scraps, each at least 3" square and totaling 2 1/3 yards
- Light print scraps, each at least 3 3/8" square and totaling 1 1/3 yards
- Dark print scraps, each at least 3 3/8" square and totaling 1 1/3 yards
- Dark print scraps, each at least 2" x 6" and totaling 2 1/4 yards
- Light print scraps, each at least 2" x 6" and totaling 2 1/4 yards
- 1/4 yard light print
- 2 1/2 yards black
- 8 yards backing fabric
- 94" x 109" piece of batting

CUTTING
For the blocks:
- Cut 360: 3" squares, light print
- Cut 120: 3 3/8" squares, light print
- Cut 360: 3" squares, dark print
- Cut 120: 3 3/8" squares, dark print
- Cut 120: 3" squares, black
Also:
- Cut 228: 2" x 6" strips, assorted light and dark prints for the pieced border
- Cut 4: 6" squares, light print, for the corner squares
- Cut 9: 2" x 44" strips, black, for the inner border
- Cut 11: 2 1/2" x 44" strips, black, for the binding

DIRECTIONS
- Draw a diagonal line from corner to corner on the wrong side of each 3 3/8" light print square.
- Place a marked light print square on a 3 3/8" dark print square, right sides together. Stitch 1/4" away from the diagonal line

on both sides, as shown. Make 120.

- Cut the squares on the drawn lines to yield 240 pieced squares.
- Lay out 2 pieced squares, three 3" light print squares, three 3" dark print squares, and one 3" black square in 3 rows of 3, as shown.

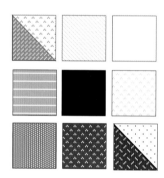

- Stitch the squares into rows and join the rows to complete a block. Make 120.
- Referring to the quilt photo for placement, lay out the blocks in 12 rows of 10.
- Stitch the blocks into rows. Join the rows.
- Cut one 2" x 44" black strip in half to yield two 2" x 22" strips.
- Stitch two 2" x 44" black strips and one 2" x 22" black strip together, end to end, to make a long inner border. Make 2.
- Measure the length of the quilt. Trim the long inner borders to that measurement and stitch them to the long sides of the quilt.
- Stitch two 2" x 44" black strips together, end to end, to make a short inner border. Make 2.
- Measure the width of the quilt, including the borders. Trim the short inner borders to that measurement and stitch them to the remaining sides of the quilt.
- Stitch sixty-two 2" x 6" print strips,

long sides together, to make a long pieced border. Make 2.

- Stitch the long pieced borders to the long sides of the quilt.
- In the same manner, stitch fifty-two 2" x 6" print strips together, to make a short pieced border. Make 2.
- Stitch a 6" light print corner square to each end of a short pieced border. Make 2.

- Stitch the short pieced borders to the remaining sides of the quilt.
- Finish as described in the *General Directions,* using the 2 1/2" x 44" black strips for the binding.

Delve into your fabric stash to make your own version of this quick-to-stitch quilt by Margot Cohen of Cedarhurst, New York. Black central squares contrast sharply with most of the scraps, creating a grid-like pattern within the Barn-Raising set of **"My Consolation"** *(90" x 105").*

My Stars!

Color value is an important element in this scrappy quilt.

QUILT SIZE: 81 1/2" x 93 1/2" including Prairie Points
BLOCK SIZE: 12" square

MATERIALS
- Assorted scraps of light, medium, and dark prints totaling 8 yards
- 2 1/3 yards ecru print for the border
- 5 1/2 yards backing fabric
- 86" x 98" piece of batting

CUTTING
Pattern pieces A, B, and C on page 28 include a 1/4" seam allowance as do all dimensions given. Pattern piece D does not need a seam allowance. Use pattern piece D to make a cutting template. Group the pieces for each block as you cut them. We recommend making a sample block before cutting pieces for the entire quilt.

For each of 15 dark blocks:
- Cut 4: 4 1/2" squares, assorted medium or dark prints in one color family
- Cut 4: A, assorted medium or dark prints in the same color family
- Cut 1: 4 1/2" square, light print
- Cut 4: B, assorted light prints in the same color family
- Cut 4: BR, light prints to match the B's

For each of 15 light blocks:
- Cut 4: 4 1/2" squares, assorted light and medium prints in one color family
- Cut 4: A, assorted light and medium prints in the same color family
- Cut 1: 4 1/2" square, dark print
- Cut 4: B, assorted dark prints in the same color family
- Cut 4: BR, dark prints to match the B's

Also:
- Cut 24: C, assorted light prints
- Cut 24: CR, assorted light prints
- Cut 16: C, assorted dark prints
- Cut 16: CR, assorted dark prints
- Cut 166: 3 3/4" squares, assorted light, medium, and dark prints, for the Prairie Points

- Cut 2: 9 1/2" x 80" lengthwise strips, ecru print, for the border
- Cut 2: 9 1/2" x 74" lengthwise strips, ecru print, for the border

DIRECTIONS
For each of 15 dark blocks:
- Stitch a light print B and a matching light print BR to a medium or dark print A to make a pieced square, as shown. Make 4.
- Lay out the pieced squares, a 4 1/2" light print square, and four 4 1/2" medium or dark print squares in 3 rows of 3, as shown. Stitch them into rows and join the rows to make a dark block.

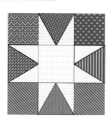

For each of 15 light blocks:
- Stitch a dark print B and a matching dark print BR to a light or medium print A to make a pieced square, as shown. Make 4.
- In the same manner as for the dark blocks, lay out the pieced squares, a 4 1/2" dark print square, and four 4 1/2" light or medium print squares. Join them to make a light block.

ASSEMBLY
- Lay out the blocks in 6 rows of 5, starting with darkest blocks at the top. Referring to the quilt photo, as desired, rearrange the blocks until you are satisfied with the color placement.
- Remove the block from the upper left corner of the layout. Place template D on the lower right corner of the block, align-

ing the corners, as shown. Draw a line along the edge of the template. Trim on the drawn line.

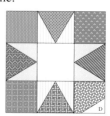

- Stitch a light print C to the corner of the block, as shown. Return the block to the layout.

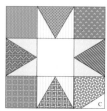

- Remove the second block from the first row of the layout. Place template D on the lower right corner and trim as before. Place template D on the lower left corner, as shown, and trim.

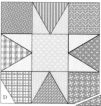

- Stitch a light print C to each trimmed corner, as shown. Return the block to the layout.

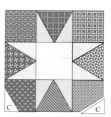

- Referring to the quilt photo, continue to remove one block at a time from the layout, and use template D to trim the appropriate corners, flipping the D template as

Full-size cutting template for My Stars. (Pattern pieces A, B, & C are on page 28.)

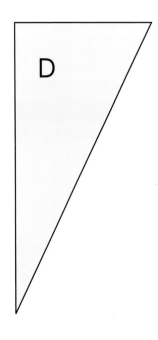

D

Margaret Peyton of Charleston, South Carolina, used an assortment of 5" fabric sample squares to make **"My Stars!"** (81 1/2" x 93 1/2"). Triangles in the corners of the blocks form little stars at the intersections of the blocks. She says, "What a study of color and value this quilt became!" Enjoy making your own color study by selecting favorite fabrics from your stash for this dynamic design.

necessary to trim each corner at the correct angle. Stitch print C's and CR's to the trimmed corners of the blocks. NOTE: *The C's and CR's will form small stars between the blocks.*

• After all block have been returned to the layout, stitch the blocks into rows and join the rows.

• Measure the length of the quilt. Trim the 9 1/2" x 74" ecru print strips to that measurement. Stitch them to the long sides of the quilt.

• Measure the width of the quilt, including the borders. Trim the 9 1/2" x 80" ecru print strips to that measurement. Stitch them to the remaining sides of the quilt.

• Layer and baste the quilt top, batting,

and backing. Quilt as desired to within 3/4" of the edges of the quilt.

• Trim the batting even with the edges of the quilt top. Trim the backing 1/4" beyond the edges of the quilt top and batting.

For the Prairie Points:

• Fold a 3 3/4" print square in half diagonally, right side out. Fold it in half again to make a Prairie Point, as shown. Press the folds. Make 166.

• Lay 39 Prairie Points along one short side of the quilt, aligning the raw edges and tucking each new Prairie Point inside the previous one.

• Keeping the backing free, pin the Prairie Points to the quilt top and batting. Stitch them to the quilt top and batting.

• In the same manner, stitch 39 Prairie Points to the remaining short side of the quilt and 44 to each of the long sides.

• Turn the Prairie Points to the outside and lightly press the edges of the quilt.

• Turn the edge of the backing under 1/2" toward the inside of the quilt. Blind-stitch it to the backside of the Prairie Points, covering the line of stitching.

Postage Stamp

Strip-piecing makes sewing the ten thousand-plus 1" squares in this quilt easier than you think!

QUILT SIZE: 93" x 111"
BLOCK SIZE: 13" square

MATERIALS
• Assorted light print and light solid strips, each at least 1 1/2" x 44" and equal to a total of 10 yards
• Assorted green, red, blue, purple, orange, brown, gold, and pink print and dark solid strips, each at least 1 1/2"-wide, ranging in length from 13" to 25", and equal to 1 1/3 yards of each color group
• 1 yard muslin
• 8 1/2" yards backing fabric
• 97" x 115" piece of batting

CUTTING
From the light prints and light solids:
• Cut 109: 1 1/2" assorted squares
• Cut 15: 1 1/2" x 20" assorted strips
• Cut 214: 1 1/2" x 44" assorted strips
From the dark color groups:
Cut 71: 1 1/2" assorted squares
From each of the 8 dark color groups:
• Cut 19: 1 1/2" x 25" strips
• Cut 20: 1 1/2" x 19" strips
• Cut 9: 1 1/2" x 13" strips
From each of 5 dark color groups:
• Cut 15: 1 1/2" x 4" strips
Also:
• Cut 13: 2 1/2" x 44" strips, muslin, for the binding

DIRECTIONS
For the light pieced strips:
• Stitch three 1 1/2" x 44" assorted light strips together to make a 3-strip panel, as shown. Make 5.
• Cut one hundred twenty 1 1/2" slices from the 3-strip panels. Set them aside.
• Stitch five 1 1/2" x 44" assorted light strips together to make a 5-strip panel. Make 6.
• Cut one hundred sixty-eight 1 1/2" slices form the 5-strip panels. Set them aside.

• Stitch seven 1 1/2" x 44" assorted light strips together to make a 7-strip panel. Make 3.
• Cut eighty-four 1 1/2" slices from the 7-strip panels. Set them aside.
• Stitch nine 1 1/2" x 44" assorted light strips together to make a 9-strip panel. Make 6.
• Cut one hundred fifty-six 1 1/2" slices from the 9-strip panels. Set them aside.
• Stitch eleven 1 1/2" x 44" assorted light strips together to make an 11-strip panel. Make 5.
• Cut one hundred thirty-two 1 1/2" slices from the 11-strip panels. Set them aside.
• Stitch thirteen 1 1/2" x 44" assorted light strips together to make a 13-strip panel. Make 3.
• Cut seventy 1 1/2" slices from the 13-strip panels. Set them aside.
• Stitch fifteen 1 1/2" x 20" assorted light strips together to make a 15-strip panel.
• Cut twelve 1 1/2" slices from the 15-strip panels. Set them aside.

For the dark pieced strips:
Follow the directions below for each of the 8 dark color groups. Use assorted prints, and solids but in the same color group, for each panel.
• Stitch three 1 1/2" x 25" assorted dark strips together to make a 3-strip panel.
• Cut one hundred twenty 1 1/2" slices from the 3-strip panels. Set them aside.
• Stitch five 1 1/2" x 25" assorted dark strips together to make a 5-strip panel.
• Cut one hundred twenty 1 1/2" slices from the 5-strip panels. Set them aside.
• Stitch seven 1 1/2" x 19" assorted dark strips together to make a 7-strip panel.
• Cut seventy-two 1 1/2" slices from the 7-strip panels. Set them aside.
• Stitch nine 1 1/2" x 13" assorted dark strips together to make a 9-strip panel.
• Cut one hundred eight 1 1/2" slices from the 9-strip panels. Set them aside.
• Stitch eleven 1 1/2" x 25" assorted dark

strips together to make an 11-strip panel.
• Cut one hundred twenty 1 1/2" slices from the 11-strip panels. Set them aside.
• Stitch thirteen 1 1/2" x 19" assorted dark strips together to make a 13-strip panel.
• Cut seventy-two 1 1/2" slices from the 13-strip panels. Set them aside.

Follow the directions below for each of 5 dark color groups. Use assorted prints and solids, but same color groups for each panel.
• Stitch fifteen 1 1/2" x 4" assorted dark strips together to make a 15-strip panel.
• Cut ten 1 1/2" slices from the 15-strip panels. Set them aside.

For each of twenty-four 13" light blocks:
• Stitch a 1 1/2" dark square between two 1 1/2" light squares to make a pieced row, as shown.
• Stitch the pieced row between two 3-square light strips to make a pieced square, as shown.
• Stitch the pieced square between two 3-square same color dark strips to make a pieced rectangle, as shown.
• Stitch the pieced rectangle between two 5-square same color dark strips, to make a pieced square, as shown.
• Stitch two 5-square light strips together to make a double row, as shown. Make 2.
• Stitch the pieced square between the double rows to make a pieced unit, as shown.

• Stitch two 9-square light strips together to make a double row. Make 2.
• Stitch the pieced unit between the dou-

(Continued on page 27)

Carolyn Zister of Waterloo, Ontario, individually cut over ten-thousand 1 1/2" squares for her **"Postage Stamp"** *(93" x 111") quilt. With strip-piecing methods, the construction of your extraordinary quilt becomes a 'piece of cake.'*

Schoolhouse

Use traditional piecing to stitch a replica of yesteryear.

QUILT SIZE: 52" x 62"
BLOCK SIZE: 9 1/2" x 10"

MATERIALS
- 2 1/4 yards tan print
- 1 1/4 yards red print
- 1 yard blue plaid NOTE: *This is the amount needed for pieced borders. If you wish to cut continuous lengthwise strips, you will need 2 yards.*
- 2 yards navy
- 3 1/2 yards backing fabric
- 56" x 66" piece of batting

CUTTING
The pattern pieces are on page 29. Pattern pieces A through D are full size and include a 1/4" seam allowance. The bell appliqué pattern is full size and does not include a turn-under allowance. Make a template of the bell pattern piece and trace around it on the right side of the fabric. Add a 1/8" to 3/16" turn-under allowance when cutting the fabric pieces out. All other dimensions include a 1/4" seam allowance. Cut the lengthwise tan and navy strips before cutting other pieces from the same yardage.

For 12 Schoolhouse blocks:
- Cut 48: 1 5/8" x 2" rectangles, tan print, for the windows
- Cut 12: 2" x 3 5/8" strips, tan print, for the doors
- Cut 12: 7/8" x 5 1/2" strips, tan print
- Cut 12: 7/8" x 6 1/8" strips, tan print
- Cut 24: 1 3/4" x 2 1/2" rectangles, tan print
- Cut 12: 1 3/4" x 4" strips, tan print
- Cut 12: 1 1/4" x 3 1/2" strips, tan print
- Cut 12: 1 1/4" x 8 1/2" strips, tan print
- Cut 12: A, tan print
- Cut 12: AR, tan print
- Cut 12: C, tan print
- Cut 12: bells, tan print
- Cut 12: 1 1/8" x 5 1/8" strips, red print
- Cut 36: 7/8" x 2" strips, red print
- Cut 48: 1 1/2" x 2" rectangles, red print
- Cut 24: 1 1/2" x 5 1/8" strips, red print
- Cut 12: 2" squares, red print
- Cut 24: 1 3/4" x 5 1/2" strips, red print
- Cut 12: B, red print
- Cut 24: 1 3/4" squares, red print

- Cut 12: D, blue plaid
- Cut 12: 1 1/4" x 2" rectangles, blue plaid

Also:
- Cut 2: 2 1/2" x 50" lengthwise strips, tan print
- Cut 5: 2 1/2" x 36" strips, tan print
- Cut 8: 2 1/2" x 10" strips, tan print
- Cut 4: 2" x 33" strips, blue plaid, for the inner border
- Cut 4: 2" x 28" strips, blue plaid, for the inner border
- Cut 2: 5 1/2" x 64" lengthwise strips, navy, for the outer border
- Cut 4: 2 1/2" x 64" lengthwise strips, navy, for the binding
- Cut 2: 5 1/2" x 54" lengthwise strips, navy, for the outer border

DIRECTIONS

For each of 12 Schoolhouse blocks:
- Stitch a 1 5/8" x 2" tan print rectangle to a 1 1/2" x 2" red print rectangle, right sides together along their length, to make a pieced rectangle. Make 4.
- Stitch a 7/8" x 2" red print strip between 2 pieced rectangles to make a window strip, as shown. Make 2.
- Stitch a 1 1/8" x 5 1/8" red print strip between two window strips to make a pieced section.

- Stitch the pieced section between two 1 1/2" x 5 1/8" red print strips to make a window unit.

- Stitch a 7/8" x 6 1/8" tan print strip to the top of the window unit to complete a window

section. Set it aside.
- Stitch a 2" x 3 5/8" tan print strip between a 7/8" x 2" red print strip and a 2" red print square to make a door strip.
- Stitch the door strip between two 1 3/4" x 5 1/2" red print strips to make a door unit.

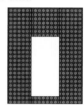

- Stitch a 7/8" x 5 1/2" tan print strip to the right side of the door unit to make a door section, as shown. Set it aside.

- Stitch a tan print C between a red print B and a blue plaid D to make a roof unit, as shown.

- Stitch the roof unit between a tan print A and AR to make a roof section, as shown. Set it aside.

- Stitch a 1 3/4" x 4" tan print strip between two 1 3/4" red print squares to make a chimney/bell-tower strip, as shown.
- Stitch a chimney/bell-tower strip between two 1 3/4" x 2 1/2" tan print rectangles to make a chimney/bell-tower unit, as shown. Set it aside.

Here's a classic quilt that will be enjoyed by your family for a lifetime. Glendora Hutson of Contoocook, New Hampshire, took an old-time favorite block and added a bell tower and appliquéd bell to create her beautiful **"Schoolhouse"** *(52" x 62") quilt. She then quilted the alphabet and numbers in the border to carry the quilt's theme to the finish.*

• Place a 1 1/4" x 3 1/2" tan print strip on a 1 1/4" x 2" blue plaid rectangle, right sides together and aligning the left edges. Mark a diagonal line and stitch on that line, as shown. Trim 1/4" beyond the stitching, open the unit and press the seam allowance toward the blue plaid.

• In the same manner, place, mark, and stitch a 1 1/4" x 8 1/2" tan print strip to the opposite end of the blue plaid rectangle. Trim 1/4" beyond the stitching and press the seam allowance toward the blue plaid to make a pieced unit.

• Stitch the pieced unit to the chimney/bell-tower unit making sure the blue plaid triangle is centered over a red square. Trim the ends of the pieced unit even with the chimney/bell-tower unit, as shown, to complete a chimney/bell-tower section.

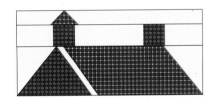

• Stitch the chimney/bell-tower section to the roof section to make the top half of the block.

• Stitch the door section to the window section to make the lower half of the block.

• Stitch the top half to the lower half of the block to complete a Schoolhouse block. Make 12.

• Needleturn appliqué a bell in the center of each bell tower, referring to the quilt photo for placement.

Assembly

• Stitch 3 Schoolhouse blocks and two 2 1/2" x 10" tan print strips together to make a pieced row, as shown. Make 4.

• Measure the rows and trim five 2 1/2" x 36" tan print strips to that measurement.

• Stitch a trimmed strip to the bottom of each pieced row.

• Referring to the quilt photo, lay out the pieced rows and stitch them together.

• Stitch the remaining trimmed strip to the top of the quilt to complete the quilt center.

• Measure the length of the quilt and trim the 2 1/2" x 50" tan print strips to that measurement. Stitch them to the sides of the quilt.

• Stitch two 2" x 28" blue plaid strips together, end to end, to make a short blue plaid strip. Make 2.

• Stitch two 2" x 33" blue plaid strips together, end to end, to make a long blue plaid strip. Make 2.

• Stitch a short blue plaid strip to a 5 1/2" x 54" navy strip, along their length, to make a short pieced border. Make 2.

• Stitch a long blue plaid strip to a 5 1/2" x 64" navy strip, along their length, to make a long pieced border. Make 2.

• Center and stitch the short pieced borders to the top and bottom of the quilt, placing the blue plaid strip against the quilt. Start, stop, and backstitch 1/4" from the edges of the quilt.

• In the same manner, center and stitch the long pieced borders to the sides of the quilt.

• Miter the corners as described in the *General Directions.*

• Finish the quilt as described in the *General Directions,* using the 2 1/2" x 64" navy strips for the binding.

(The full-size pattern pieces are on page 29.)

Stars All Around

Make a quilt that's the star of the show!

QUILT SIZE: 88" x 112"
BLOCK SIZE: 12" square

MATERIALS

• Assorted dark print scraps for the stars and block corners
• 1/4 yard each of 18 assorted light prints for the star backgrounds
• 3 3/4 yards gray print
• 4 3/4 yards black plaid
• 2 yards red print
• 8 yards backing fabric
• 92" x 116" piece of batting

CUTTING

The pattern pieces are on pages 30-31. Pattern pieces are full size and include a 1/4" seam allowance, as do all dimensions given. We recommend making a sample block before cutting fabric for the entire quilt. Cut the lengthwise black plaid strips before cutting other pieces from the same yardage.

For each of 18 Star blocks:

• Cut 1 each of pieces B, D, E, F, G, and J, assorted dark prints in one color family, for the star
• Cut 4: L, assorted dark prints in one color family, for the block corners
• Cut 1 each of pieces A, C, H, I, and K, one light print, for the star's background

For the pieced border:

• Cut 228: 3 1/2" squares, gray print
• Cut 2: 6 7/8" squares, gray print
• Cut 112: 3 1/2" x 6 1/2" rectangles, black plaid
• Cut 2: 6 7/8" squares, black plaid

Also:

• Cut 2: 13 1/4" squares, gray print
• Cut 8: 12 7/8" squares, gray print, then cut 2 of them in half diagonally to yield 4 large triangles
• Cut 2: 5" x 98" lengthwise strips, black plaid, for the inner border
• Cut 2: 5" x 74"lengthwise strips, black plaid, for the inner border
• Cut 6: 12 7/8" squares, black plaid
• Cut 2: 13 1/4" squares, black plaid
• Cut 19: 2" x 44" strips, red print

• Cut 11: 2 1/2" x 44" strips, red print, for the binding

PIECING

For each of 18 Star blocks:

• Stitch a dark print B between a light print A and a light print C, as shown.
• Stitch a dark print E between a dark print D and F, as shown.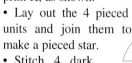
• Stitch a dark print G to a light print H, as shown.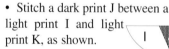
• Stitch a dark print J between a light print I and light print K, as shown.
• Lay out the 4 pieced units and join them to make a pieced star.
• Stitch 4 dark print L's together, as shown, back-stitching to secure the ends of each seam.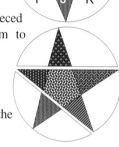

• To complete the block, stitch the pieced star to the L unit in either of the following ways:

  1. Turn the edge of the star unit under on the 1/4" seamline and appliqué it to the L unit.

  2. Fold the pieced star in half, then in half again. Make a mark on the edge of the unit at each fold. Align and pin the seamlines of the L unit to the marks on the star unit, right sides together. Stitch the units together, aligning the raw edges as you go.

• Draw diagonal lines from corner to corner on the wrong side of a 13 1/4" gray print square.
• Place the marked square on a 13 1/4" black plaid square, right sides together. Stitch 1/4" away from both sides of one diagonal line, as shown. Make 2.
• Cut the squares on the drawn lines to yield 8 pieced triangles. You will use 6. Press the seam allowances toward the black plaid.
• Join 2 pieced triangles to make the center square, as shown. Set it aside.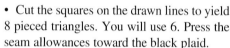
• Stitch a pieced triangle to a large gray print triangle to make a pieced square. Make 4. Set them aside.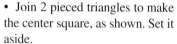
• Draw a diagonal line from corner to corner on the wrong side of each remaining 12 7/8" gray print square.
• Place a marked gray print square on a 12 7/8" black plaid square, right sides together. Stitch 1/4" away from the diagonal line on both sides. Make 6.
• Cut the squares on the drawn lines to yield 12 pieced squares. Press the seam allowances toward the black plaid. Set them aside.

For the pieced border:

• Draw a diagonal line from corner to corner on the wrong side of each 3 1/2" gray print square.
• Place a marked gray print square on a 3 1/2" x 6 1/2" black plaid rectangle, right sides together. Stitch on the drawn line, as shown. Open the gray print square and press it toward the corner, aligning the outer edges. Trim the seam allowance to 1/4".
• Place a marked 3 1/2" gray print square on the opposite end of the black plaid rectangle, right sides together. Stitch on the marked line. Press and trim as before to complete a pieced rectangle. Make 56.

*If you're a fan of the country look, you'll want to make this striking quilt. Nelda Paolini of Wyomissing, Pennsylvania, designed a unique setting for a five-point traditional Star of the West block in "**Stars All Around**" (88" x 112").*

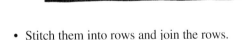

• Make a pieced rectangle, changing the direction of the stitching lines, as shown. Make 56.

• Stitch 2 pieced rectangles together to make a border unit. Make 56.
• Stitch 12 border units together to make a short pieced border. Make 2.

• In the same manner, stitch 16 border units together to make a long pieced border. Make 2. Set them aside.
• Draw a diagonal line on the wrong side of each 6 7/8" gray print square.
• Place a marked gray print square on a 6 7/8" black plaid square, right sides together. Stitch 1/4" away from the diagonal line on both sides. Make 2.
• Cut the squares on the drawn lines to yield 4 pieced squares.
• Draw a diagonal line on the wrong side of each remaining 3 1/2" gray print square. Place a marked square on the black plaid half of a pieced square and stitch on the drawn line.
• Open the square and press it toward the corner, aligning the outer edges. Trim the seam allowance to 1/4" to complete a corner unit. Make 4.

ASSEMBLY
• Referring to the quilt photo, lay out the Star blocks, center square, and pieced squares in 7 rows of 5.

• Stitch them into rows and join the rows.
• Stitch nine 2" x 44" red print strips together, end to end, to make a pieced strip.
• Cut two 98" lengths and two 74" lengths from the pieced strip.
• Stitch a 2" x 98" red print strip to a 5" x 98" black plaid strip, right sides together along their length, to make a long border strip. Make 2.
• Stitch a 2" x 74" red print strip to a 5" x 74" black plaid strip in the same manner, to make a short border strip. Make 2.
• Center and stitch the short border strips to the short sides of the quilt, placing the black plaid strip against the quilt. Start and stop stitching 1/4" from each end and backstitch.
• Stitch the long border strips to the long sides of the quilt in the same manner.
• Miter the corners as described in the *General Directions.*
• Referring to the quilt photo, stitch the long pieced borders to the long sides of the quilt.

• Stitch a corner unit to each end of the short pieced borders.
• Stitch the short pieced borders to the remaining sides of the quilt.
• Stitch the remaining 2" x 44" red print strips together, end to end, to make a pieced strip.
• Cut two 2" x 108 1/2" lengths and two 87 1/2" lengths from the pieced strip.
• Stitch the 2" x 108 1/2" red print strips to the long sides of the quilt.
• Stitch the 87 1/2" red print strips to the remaining sides of the quilt.
• Finish the quilt as described in the *General Directions,* using the 2 1/2" x 44" red print strips for the binding.

(The full-size pattern pieces are on pages 30-31.)

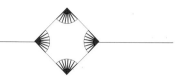

Tarzan's Railroad Quilt

Make a replica of this extraordinary heirloom quilt.

QUILT SIZE: 75" x 98"
BLOCK SIZE: 18" square

MATERIALS
- 3 yards red
- Scrap of yellow at least 10" x 12 1/2"
- 2 3/4 yards turquoise
- 1 1/8 yards black
- 8 1/2 yards muslin
- 5 3/4 yards backing fabric
- 79" x 102" piece of batting
- Paper for the foundations

NOTE: *The quiltmaker cut sashing strips and cornerstone blocks in half for the top and bottom of her quilt. The following directions are for complete cornerstone blocks and sashings.*

CUTTING
The pattern pieces are on pages 25 and 26. Appliqué pattern D is full size and does not include a seam allowance. Make a template of the pattern piece. Trace around the template on the right side of the fabric and add a 1/8" to 3/16" turn-under allowance when cutting the pieces out. Pattern piece C is full size and includes a 1/4" seam allowance as do all dimensions given. Fabric for the foundation piecing will be cut as you stitch the blocks. Each piece must be at least 1/2" larger on all sides than the section it will cover. Refer to the General Directions *as needed.*

- Cut 9: 2 1/2" x 44" strips, red, for the binding
- Cut 48: C, red
- Cut 20: D, yellow
- Cut 50: 1 3/8" x 40" strips, turquoise
- Cut 10: 2" x 40" strips, turquoise
- Cut 62: 3/4" x 18 1/2" strips, black
- Cut 55: 1 1/8" x 40" strips, muslin
- Cut 12: 18 1/2" squares, muslin

DIRECTIONS
Follow the foundation piecing instructions .in the General Directions *to piece the foundations.*

- Trace the full-size foundation patterns on the foundation paper, transferring all lines and numbers and leaving a 1" space between foundations. Make 48 foundation A's and 20 foundation B's. Cut each one out 1/2" beyond the broken line. Piece each foundation in numerical order.

For each Foundation A:
- Use the following fabrics in these positions:
  - 1 - red
  - 2 - muslin
  - 3 - red
  - 4 - muslin

Continue in this manner, alternating red and muslin.
- Trim each foundation on the broken lines.

For each Foundation B:
- Cut the foundation on the line between #1 and #32. When beginning to piece the foundation at position #1, keep the other end out of the way. Be certain the fabrics for positions #1 and 32 extend 1/2" beyond the cut edges of the foundation.
- Use the following fabrics in these positions:
  - 1 - muslin
  - 2 - red
  - 3 - muslin
  - 4 - red

Continue in this manner, alternating red and muslin.
- Trim the #1 and #32 fabrics 1/4" beyond the cut edges of the foundations. Trim the curved edge and the outer straight edges of the foundations on the broken lines.
- Stitch the cut edge of the #1 fabric and the #32 fabric together to make a square, as shown. Repeat for each of the remaining foundation B's.
- Appliqué a yellow D to the center of each foundation B. Set them aside.

For the blocks:
- Carefully remove the paper from a completed foundation A.
- Press the curved seam allowance of a red C toward the wrong side. Pin the C to the foundation A. Appliqué the pressed edge to the foundation.
- Press the long curved seam allowance of the foundation A to the wrong side.
- Pin the foundation to one corner of an 18 1/2" muslin square, aligning the straight edges, as shown.

- Appliqué the curved edge to the square. Repeat for the remaining corners of the square to complete a block. Make 12.
- Turn a block wrong side up. To reduce bulk, trim the corners of the muslin square 1/4" from the appliqué stitches of the Foundation A. Repeat for the remaining blocks.

For the Railroad Track sashing:
- Stitch eleven 1 1/8" x 40" muslin strips and ten 1 3/8" x 40" turquoise strips into a panel. Stitch a 2" x 40" turquoise strip to each long side of the panel. Make 5. Press the seam allowances toward the turquoise. Cut thirty-one 5 1/2"-wide pieced sashings from the panels.
- Trim each pieced sashing to 18 1/2", trimming equal amounts from the wide

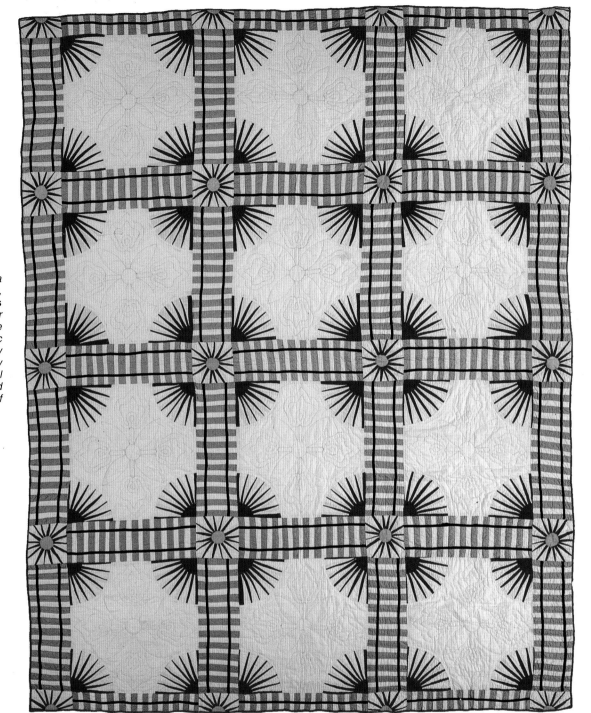

*Around the year 1935, Victoria Guillaume of Damar, Kansas, pieced and appliquéd **"Tarzan's Railroad Quilt"** (75" x 98") for her son Leon, who at that time worked for the Union Pacific Railroad. Her grandson, Stanley Guillaume, now owns this family heirloom. You'll use traditional piecing, foundation piecing, and appliqué to make a replica of this memorable quilt.*

turquoise strips on each end.
• Press one long edge of a 3/4" x 18 1/2" black strip 1/4" toward the wrong side.
• Lay the black strip right side down on a pieced sashing, placing the pressed edge 1" from a long edge of the sashing. Stitch 1/4" away from the unpressed edge of the black strip, as shown.
• Carefully trim 1/8"

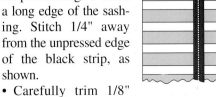

from both long edges of the black strip to reduce bulk.
• Fold the strip over the stitching and appliqué the pressed edge to the sashing.
• In the same manner, stitch, then appliqué a black strip to the opposite side of the pieced sashing to make a Railroad Track sashing. Make 31.

ASSEMBLY
• Referring to the quilt photo, lay out 4 foundation B's and 3 Railroad Track sash-

ings. Stitch them together to make a sashing row. Make 5.
• Lay out 4 Railroad Track sashings and 3 blocks. Stitch them together to make a block row. Make 4.
• Lay out the sashing rows alternately with the block rows. Join the rows to complete the quilt top.
• Finish the quilt as described in the *General Directions*, using the 2 1/2" x 44" red strips for the binding.

(The full-size pattern pieces are on pages 25-26.)

Turkey Tracks

Enjoy making this old-time favorite.

QUILT SIZE: 81" x 94"
BLOCK SIZE: 11" square

MATERIALS
• Fat quarter (18" x 22") each of 42 dark prints
• 3 yards muslin
• 3 1/2 yards print fabric for the sashing, border, and binding
• 5 1/2 yards backing fabric
• 85" x 99" piece of batting

CUTTING
Cut the lengthwise strips parallel to the selvage before cutting other pieces from the same yardage. Group the pieces for each block as you cut them. Emma did not include a top or bottom sashing on her quilt. They are included in the directions for quilter's who prefer to use them.

For each of 42 blocks:
• Cut 2: 5 1/8" squares, one dark print, then cut them in half diagonally to yield 4 large triangles
• Cut 1: 2 1/2" x 6 1/2" strip, same dark print
• Cut 2: 2 1/2" squares, same dark print
• Cut 16: 1 3/4" squares, same dark print
Also:
• Cut 168: 1 3/4" x 4" rectangles, muslin
• Cut 336: 1 3/4" x 3" rectangles, muslin
• Cut 168: 2 1/2" squares, muslin
• Cut 168: 1 3/4" squares, muslin
• Cut 7: 2 1/2" x 92" lengthwise strips, print, for the sashing and border
• Cut 2: 2 1/2" x 83" lengthwise strips, print, for the border
• Cut 36: 2 1/2" x 11 1/2" strips, print, for the sashing
• Cut 9: 2 1/2" x 44" strips, print, for the binding
PIECING
For each Turkey Tracks block:
• Stitch a 2 1/2" dark print square between two 2 1/2" muslin

squares to make a pieced strip. Make 2.
• Stitch the 2 1/2" x 6 1/2" same dark print strip between the pieced strips to make a pieced square.
• Stitch a large same print triangle to each side of the pieced square to complete a center unit. Set it aside.

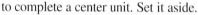

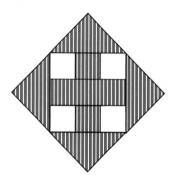

• Draw a diagonal line from corner to corner on the wrong side of each 1 3/4" same dark print square.
• Place a marked square on one end of the 1 3/4" x 3" muslin rectangle, aligning the edges. Stitch on the drawn line, as shown.
• Open the square and press it toward the corner, aligning the raw edges. Trim the seam allowance to 1/4".
• Place a marked square on the other end of the muslin rectangle. Stitch on the drawn line, as shown. Press and trim as before to complete a pieced rectangle. Make 8.

• Stitch a 1 3/4" x 4" muslin rectangle between 2 pieced rectangles to make a pieced strip, as shown. Make 4.

• Stitch a 1 3/4" muslin square to each end of 2 of the pieced strips.
• Lay out the center unit and 4 pieced strips. Join them to make a Turkey Tracks block. Make 42.

ASSEMBLY
• Lay out the blocks in 6 vertical rows of 7. Place the 2 1/2" x 11" print sashing strips between the blocks in each vertical row.
• Stitch the blocks and strips into 6 vertical rows. Press the seam allowances toward the sashing.
• Measure the rows. Trim the 2 1/2" x 92" print strips to that measurement.
• Place the trimmed strips between the rows.
• Join the rows and strips.
• Stitch the remaining trimmed strips to the long sides of the quilt.
• Measure the width of the quilt. Trim the 2 1/2" x 83" print strips to that measurement. Stitch them to the remaining sides of the quilt.
• Finish the quilt as described in the *General Directions,* using the 2 1/2" x 44" print strips for the binding.

"Turkey Tracks" *(81" x 94"   ) was pieced by Emma Fehr Hockenberger (1859-1946) and later quilted by her daughter Esther Vander Millen (1883-1970). Fabrics dating from as early as 1860 and remnants from Esther's childhood clothing make up most of the blocks. The sashing fabric was purchased in the 1920s or '30s specifically to complete this quilt which is now a treasured heirloom owned by granddaughter Zylpha Siudara of Rochester, NY.*

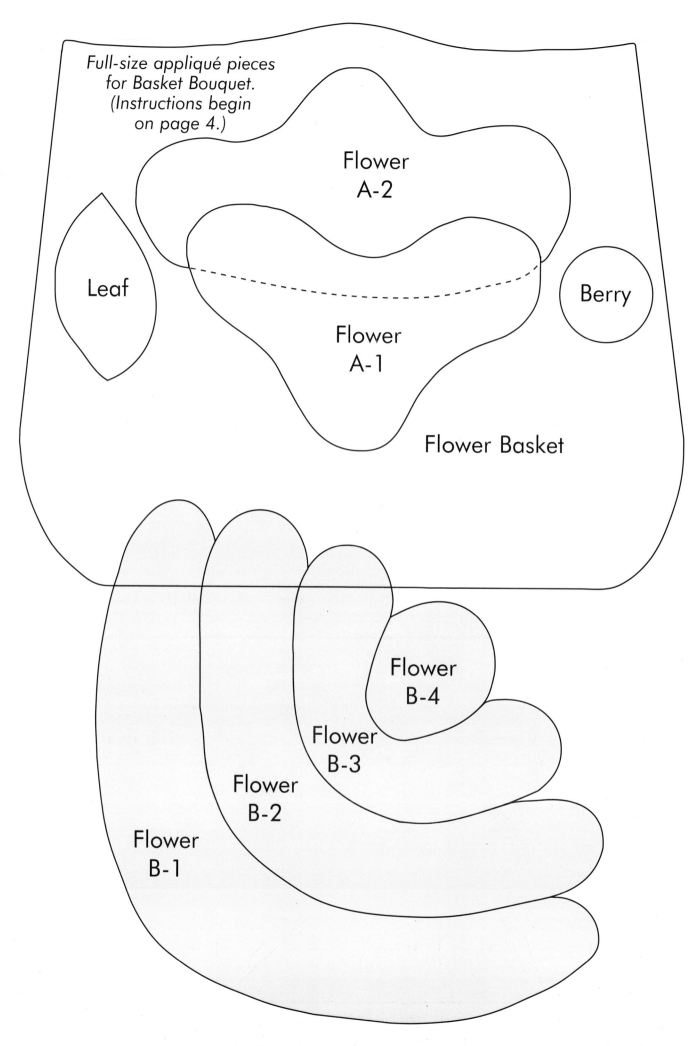

Full-size appliqué pieces for Basket Bouquet. (Instructions begin on page 4.)

Flower A-2

Leaf

Berry

Flower A-1

Flower Basket

Flower B-4

Flower B-3

Flower B-2

Flower B-1

Cabin Circles
(continued from page 7)

• Cut 5: 4 1/2" x 44" strips, blue print, for the border
• Cut 6: 2 1/2" x 44" strips, black print, for the binding

DIRECTIONS

• Stitch a 1" x 9" red print strip to a 1" x 9" light print strip, along their length, to make a pieced panel. Make 10. Press the seam allowances toward the light print strips.

• Cut eight 1" slices from each panel to yield 80 pieced units.
• Place a pieced unit on a 1" x 13" light print strip, right sides together, with the red print square toward the top.
• Stitch the unit to the strip. Place another unit right after the first one and stitch it to the strip, as before. Stitch 6 more units to the strip, as before.

• In the same manner, stitch 8 units to each of the remaining 1" x 13" light print strips. Cut them apart to yield 80 pieced units. Press the seam allow-ances toward the last strip added.
• In the same manner, stitch a pieced unit to a 1 1/2" x 13" dark print strip. Stitch a total of 8 pieced units to the strip, as before.
• Stitch 8 pieced units to each of the remaining 1 1/2" x 13" dark print strips. Cut them apart and press the seam allowances toward the last strip added.
• Continue adding strips to the sides of the 80 pieced units in the same manner, using the remaining 1 1/2"-wide dark print strips and 1"-wide light print strips, as shown.

• Lay out 4 blocks, as shown. Stitch them together in pairs and join the pairs to make a Log Cabin Circle block. Make 20.

ASSEMBLY

• Lay out the Log Cabin Circle blocks in 5 rows of 4. Stitch them into rows and join the rows.
• Stitch the 4 1/2" x 44" blue print strips together, end to end, to make a pieced strip.
• Measure the length of the quilt. Cut 2 lengths from the pieced strip each equal to that measurement. Stitch them to the long sides of the quilt.
• Measure the width of the quilt, including the borders. Trim 2 lengths from the pieced strip each equal to that measurement. Stitch them to the remaining sides of the quilt.
• Finish the quilt as described in the *General Directions,* using the 2 1/2" x 44" black print strips for the binding.

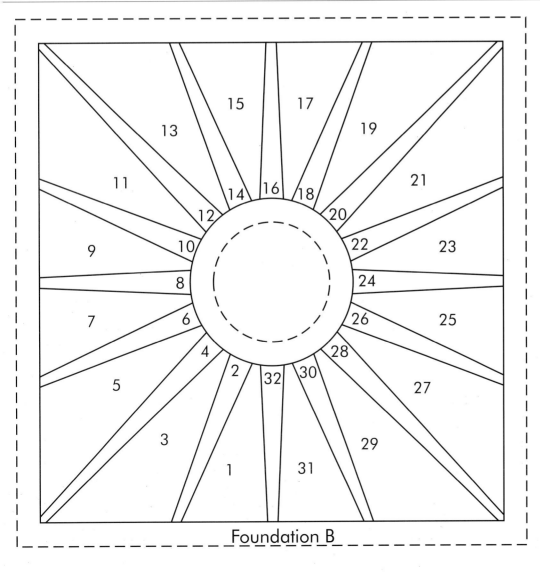

Foundation B

Full-size foundation pattern B for Tarzan's Railroad Quilt. Foundation pattern A, appliqué pattern D, and pattern piece C are on page 26. (Instructions begin on page 20.)

*Full-size foundation pattern A,
appliqué pattern D, and pattern piece C for
Tarzan's Railroad Quilt.
(Instructions begin on page 20.)*

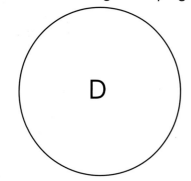

D

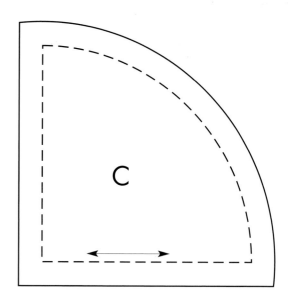

C

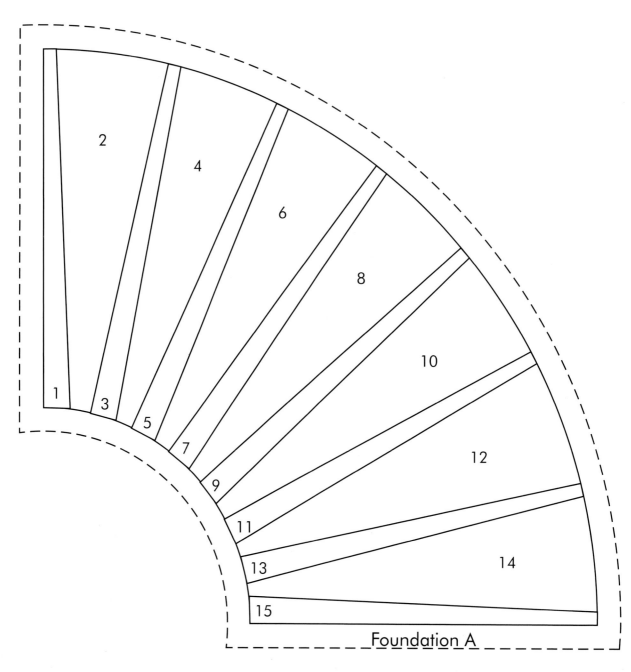

2

4

6

8

10

12

14

1

3

5

7

9

11

13

15

Foundation A

Postage Stamp
(continued from page 14)

ble rows to make a pieced square, as shown.

• Stitch the pieced square between two 9-square same color dark strips, to make a pieced unit.

• Stitch the pieced unit between two 11-square same color dark strips, to make a pieced square.

• Stitch the pieced square between two 11-square light strips to make a pieced unit.

• Stitch the pieced unit between two 13-square light strips, to complete a 13" light block, as shown.

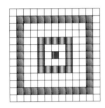

For each of twenty-five 13" dark blocks:

• In the same manner, and referring to the diagram for the number of squares in each strip and the light/dark placement, make a 13" dark block, as shown.

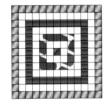

For each of six 15" light blocks:

• Referring to the diagram make a 15" light block.

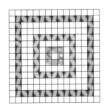

For each of five 15" dark blocks:

• Referring to the diagram make a 15" dark block.

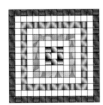

ASSEMBLY

• Lay out a 15" light block. Measure 1 1/2" along the raw edge on both sides

of a corner and make pencil marks, as shown. Measure and mark the opposite corner in the same manner.

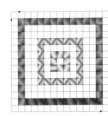

• Draw 2 diagonal lines across the block to connect the dots. Stitch 1/8" outside of each line, as shown to stabilize the bias edges.

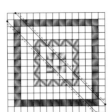

• Cut on the drawn lines to yield 2 light setting triangles. Repeat with the remaining 15" light blocks to make a total of 12 light setting triangles.

• In the same manner, mark and cut the 15" dark blocks to yield 10 dark setting triangles.

• Lay out the 13" light and dark blocks, alternating them. Fill in the sides with the light and dark setting triangles, placing dark triangles along the short sides and light ones along the long sides.

• Stitch the blocks and triangles into diagonal rows. Join the rows.

• Finish the quilt as described in the *General Directions,* using the 2 1/2" x 44" muslin strips, for the binding.

Assembly Diagram

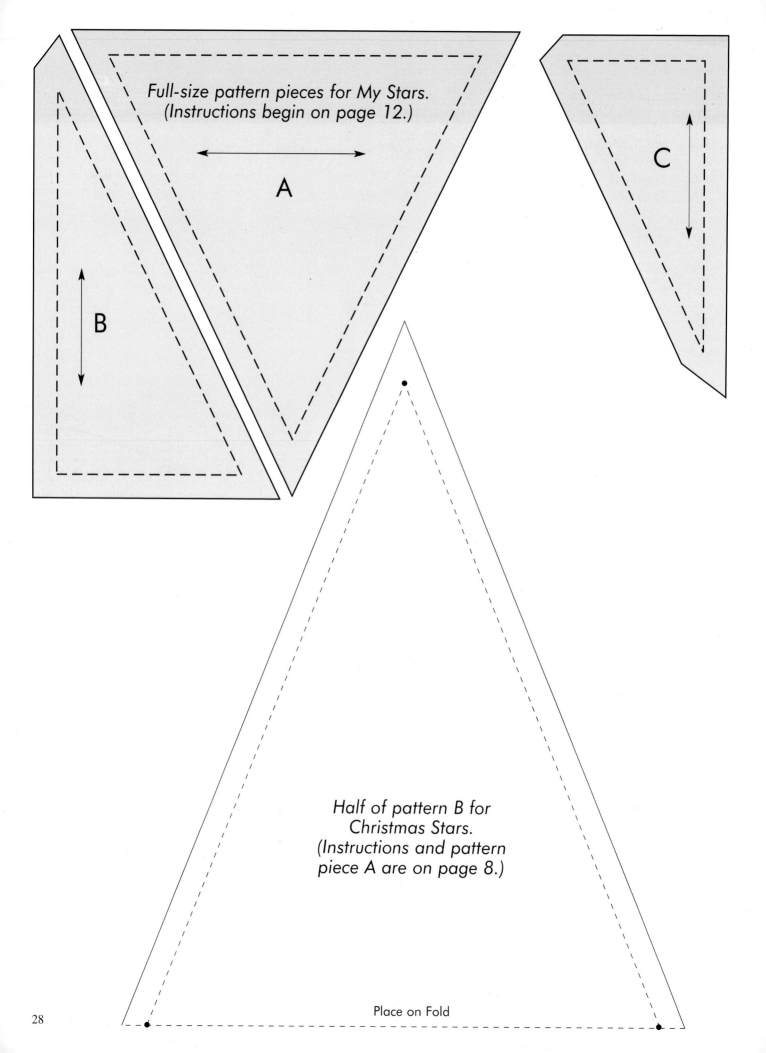

Full-size pattern pieces for My Stars.
(Instructions begin on page 12.)

A

B

C

Half of pattern B for
Christmas Stars.
(Instructions and pattern
piece A are on page 8.)

Place on Fold

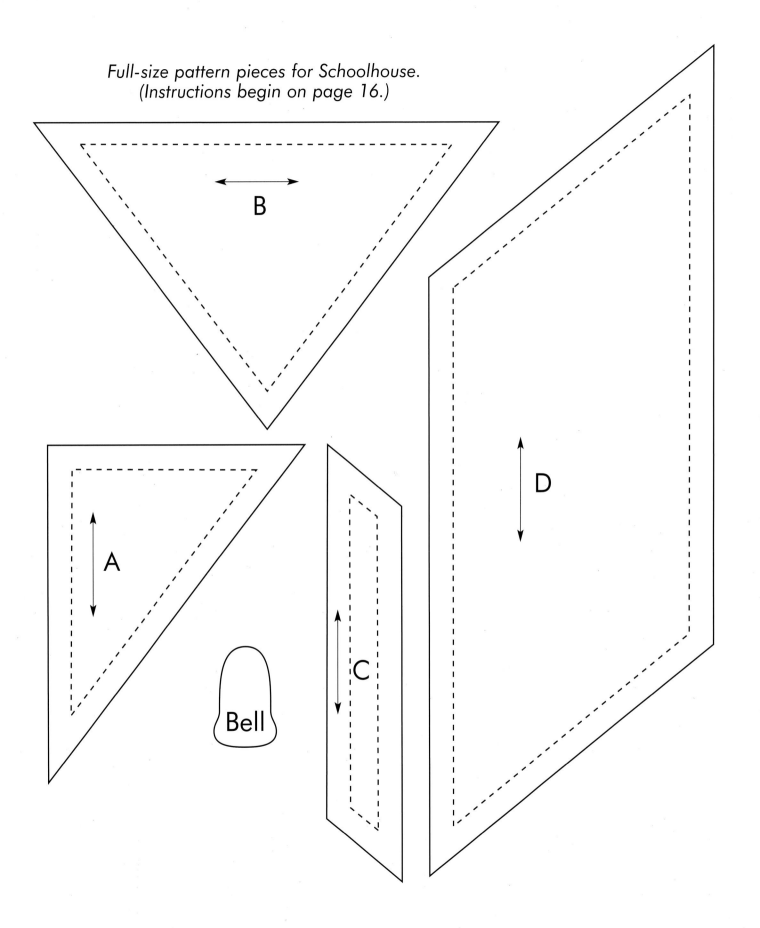

Full-size pattern pieces for Schoolhouse.
(Instructions begin on page 16.)

B

A

Bell

C

D

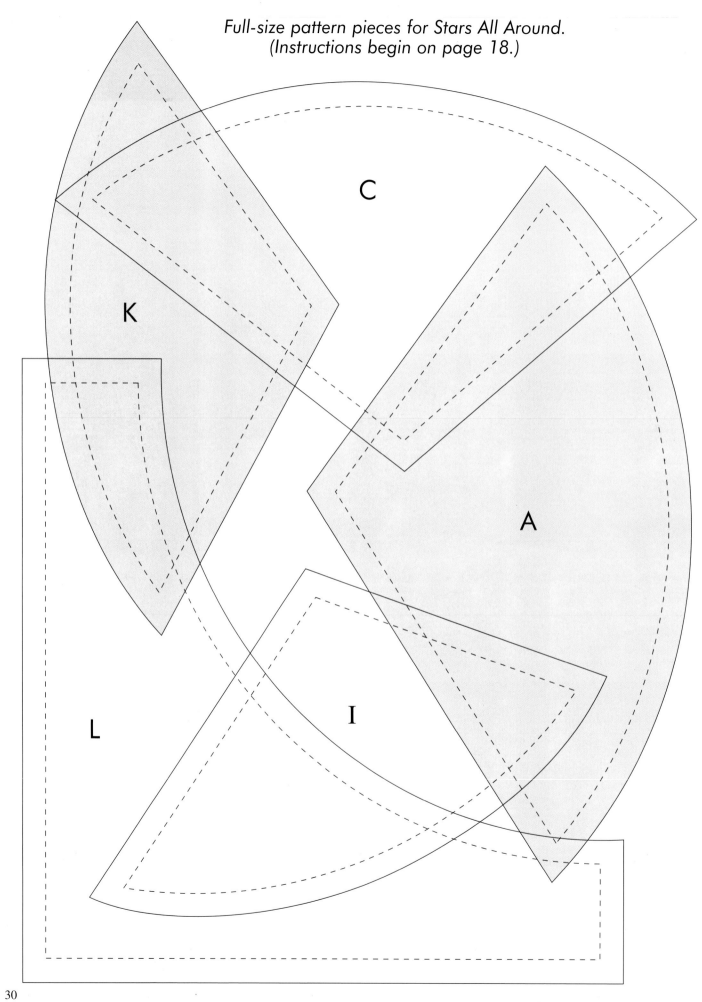

Full-size pattern pieces for Stars All Around.
(Instructions begin on page 18.)

C

K

A

L

I

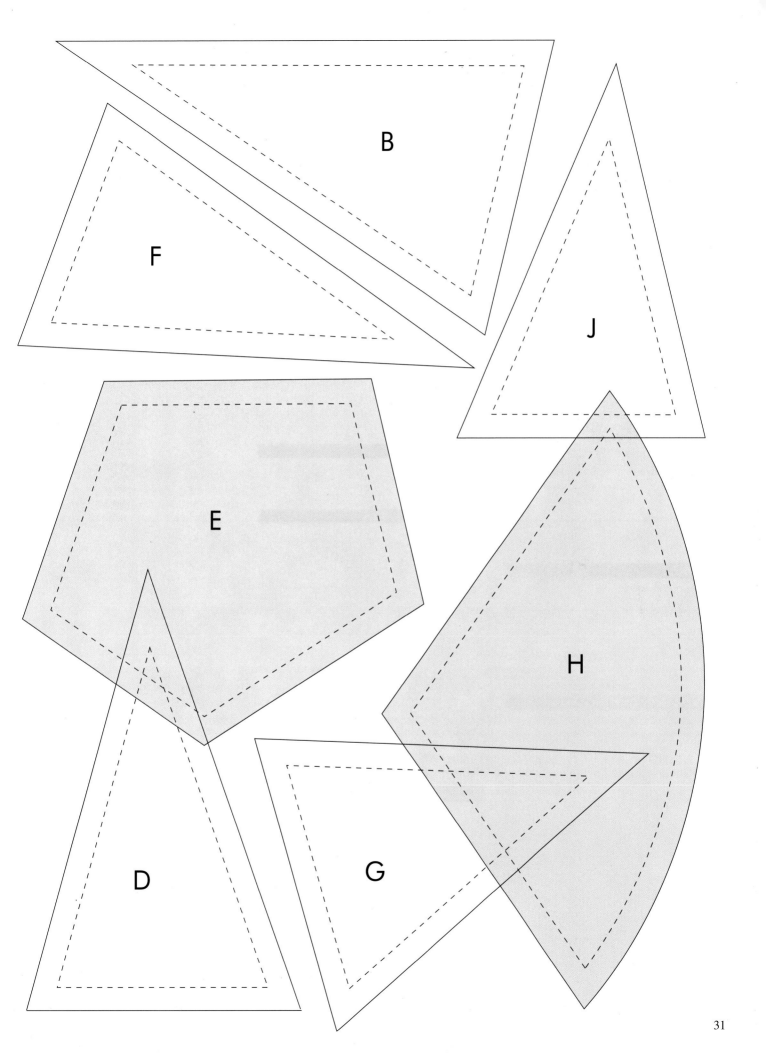

B

F

J

E

H

D

G

General Directions

Read the pattern directions before cutting fabric. Yardage requirements are based on 44" fabric with a useable width of 42". Unless otherwise noted, all dimensions include a 1/4" seam allowance.

We suggest using 100% cotton. Pre-wash fabrics in warm water with mild detergent and no fabric softener.

TEMPLATES

Template patterns are full size. The solid line is the cutting line; the dashed line is the stitching line. An "R" following the letter means the piece must be reversed. Place a sheet of clear plastic over the patterns and trace the cutting line and/or stitching line. Templates for machine piecing include seam allowances, templates for hand piecing generally do not. Templates for appliqué never include seam allowances.

MARKING FABRIC

Test marking tools for removability before using them. For machine piecing, mark the right side of the fabric. For hand piecing, mark the wrong side, and flip all asymmetrical templates before tracing them. Cut just enough pieces for a sample block and piece it to be sure your templates are accurate.

Trace appliqué templates on the right side of the fabric. Leave space between pieces to allow for a 1/8" to 3/16" turn-under allowance. For machine appliqué, cut directly on the traced line.

PIECING

For machine piecing, start and stop stitching at the cut edges unless otherwise noted.

For hand piecing, begin with a small backstitch. Continue with a small running stitch, backstitching every 3-4 stitches. Stitch directly on the marked line from seamline to seamline, not edge to edge.

FOUNDATION PIECING

For each foundation, trace all of the lines and numbers onto paper. The solid line is the stitching line and the broken line is the cutting line. The fabric pieces do not have to be cut precisely. Be generous when cutting fabric pieces as excess fabric will be trimmed away after sewing. Generally, fabric pieces should be large enough to extend 1/2" beyond the seamline on all sides before stitching.

With certain designs, the foundation pattern is the reverse of the finished block. That's because fabric pieces are placed on the unmarked side of the foundation and stitched on the marked side. Stitch the fabrics to the foundation in numerical order.

Center the first piece, right side up, over position 1 on the unmarked side of the foundation. Hold the foundation up to a light to make sure the raw edges of the fabric extend at least 1/2" beyond the seamline on all sides. Hold this first piece in place with a small dab of glue or a pin, if desired.

Place the fabric for position 2 on the first piece, right sides together. Turn the foundation over and stitch on the line between 1 and 2, extending the stitching past the beginning and end of the line by a few stitches. Trim the seam allowance to 1/4". Fold the position 2 piece right side up and press. Continue adding pieces to the foundation in the same manner until all positions are covered and the block is complete. Trim the fabric pieces even with the outer edges of the foundation.

Remove the paper when instructed to do so in the pattern. The pieces will be perforated from the stitching and can be gently pulled free.

APPLIQUÉ

Mark the position of the pieces on the background. To hand appliqué, pin the pieces to the background in stitching order. Use a blindstitch to appliqué the pieces, turning under the allowance as you stitch. Do not turn under or stitch edges that will be overlapped by other pieces.

PRESSING

Press seam allowances toward the darker of the two pieces unless instructed otherwise in the pattern.

MITERED BORDERS

Cut border strips the length specified in the pattern. Match the center of the quilt top with the center of the border and pin. Stitch, beginning, ending, and backstitching each seamline 1/4" from the edge of the quilt top. After all borders have been attached, miter one corner at a time. With the quilt top right side down, lay one border over the other. Draw a straight line at a 45° angle from the inner to the outer corner.

Reverse the positions of the borders, and mark another corner-to-corner line. With the borders right sides together and the marked seamlines carefully matched, stitch from the inner to the outer corner. Trim the excess fabric, and press the seam open.

FINISHING YOUR QUILT

Mark the quilt top before basting it together with the batting and backing. Then, tape the backing, wrong side up, on a flat surface to anchor it. Smooth the batting on top, followed by the quilt top, right side up. Baste the three layers together. Quilt as desired.

BINDING

Trim the excess batting and backing 1/4" beyond the raw edges of the quilt top. Cut binding strips with the grain for straight-edge quilts. To make 1/2" finished binding, cut 2 1/2"-wide strips. Stitch strips together with diagonal seams; trim and press the seams open.

Fold the strip in half lengthwise, wrong side in, and press. Position the strip on the right side of the quilt top, aligning the raw edges of the binding with the edge of the quilt top. Leaving 6" free and beginning at least 8" from one corner, stitch the binding to the quilt with a 1/2" seam allowance measuring from the raw edge of the backing. When you reach a corner, stop stitching 1/2" from the edge of the backing and backstitch. Clip the threads and remove the quilt from the machine. Fold the binding up and away from the quilt, forming a 45° angle, as shown.

Keeping the angled folds secure, fold the binding back down. This fold should be even with the edge of the quilt top. Begin stitching at the fold.

Continue stitching around the quilt in this manner to within 6" of the starting point. To finish, fold both strips back along the edge of the quilt so that the folded edges meet about 3" from both lines of stitching and the binding lies flat on the quilt. Finger press to crease the folds. Cut both strips 1 1/4" from the folds.

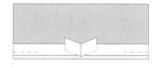

Open both strips and place the ends at right angles to each other, right sides together. Fold the bulk of the quilt out of your way. Join the strips with a diagonal seam, as shown.

Trim the seam allowance to 1/4" and press it open. Refold the strip wrong side in. Place the binding flat against the quilt and finish stitching it to the quilt. Blindstitch the binding to the back, covering the seamline and trimming the layers, if necessary, so that the binding edge will be filled with batting when you fold the binding to the back of the quilt.

Handmade by